MY FAVORITE DINOSAURS

BY JOHN SIBBICK
TEXT BY RUTH ASHBY

SCHOLASTIC INC.
New York · Toronto · London · Auckland · Sydney
Mexico City · New Delhi · Hong Kong · Buenos Aires

ISBN 0-439-82801-5

18 17 16 15 14 13 12   18 19 20 21 22/0

Printed in the U.S.A.   40

First Scholastic printing, October 2005

Editor — Howard Zimmerman

Designed by Gilda Hannah

INTRODUCTION

John Sibbick has been painting dinosaurs professionally for more than twenty years. But he has been drawing and dreaming about these fantastic animals his entire life. So when it comes to "favorites," John Sibbick has more than a few. Rather than individual dinosaurs, he loves entire groups of them. Take, for instance, the crested plant-eating dinosaurs called the "duckbills." There were many different kinds of them, and many of them had fantastic head crests, like *Parasaurolophus* and *Lambeosaurus*. Another group that has always captured his imagination are the small, fast-moving dinosaurs, such as *Ornithomimus,* which looked like an ostrich posing as a dinosaur, and *Coelophysis,* one of the earliest of the swift predators. And, like anyone else, John has always been interested in the large, ferocious meat-eaters like *Tyrannosaurus rex, Ceratosaurus,* and *Neovenator*. These are just a few of John Sibbick's favorite dinosaurs. Now, as you read through the book, it's your turn to find *your* favorite dinosaurs.

—Ruth Ashby

Iguanodon had sharp spikes on its thumbs. It used the spikes to defend itself. With its beaked mouth, it tore off leaves from trees and bushes. Then it chewed its food in its powerful jaws. *Iguanodon* could walk either on two legs or on all fours. It could use its sharp thumb spike as a weapon. Below, an *Iguanodon* stabs a meat-eater in the neck.

This *Iguanodon* herd is migrating in search of food. As the dinosaurs move through the water, they graze on reeds, ferns, and trees. A group of small plant-eaters runs through their ranks. To the right, a hungry *Neovenator* watches the herd pass by. It is waiting for one *Iguanodon* to wander off from the others. Then it will attack!

These *Maiasaura* are good parents. They are guarding nests that each hold up to twenty eggs. Some are feeding hatchlings with chewed up-leaves and berries. But even watchful parents cannot protect everyone. One tiny *Maiasaura* baby has been caught by a meat-eating lizard. Will its mother be able to save it?

Maiasaura was a kind of dinosaur called a "duckbill." Its wide, toothless mouth looked a lot like the bill of a duck. Unlike ducks, though, these dinosaurs had rows of teeth in their cheeks. They used these teeth to grind their food.

A hungry *Allosaurus* tears into a *Diplodocus*. *Allosaurus* had many weapons. It had dozens of dagger-like teeth and great claws on its hands and feet. It will use all of them to bring down this long-necked giant.

Like other huge plant-eaters, *Diplodocus* had to eat all the time to survive. It stretched its neck to graze on tall trees and high bushes. Then it gulped down its food without even chewing. Pebbles in its stomach ground up its food. Big plant-eaters swallowed small stones to help them with digestion.

A herd of giant *Apatosaurus* tramples everything in its path. One animal rears up on its hind legs to reach the very tiptop branches of a tree. By the time this herd moves on, every bit of plant food will be eaten.

Off to the side, a *Ceratosaurus* hungrily eyes the herd. If an *Apatosaurus* strays away from the others, *Ceratosaurus* will strike.

Large meat-eaters, like *Cerataurus* and the *Tyrannosaurus rex* on the bottom right, also ate other, smaller meat-eaters.

Many different kinds of duckbilled dinosaurs gather at a shallow lake to eat and drink. Some large *Parasaurolophus* graze on the right. A *Lambeosaurus* splashes its tail in the water. Striped *Corythosaurus* rest on the sand. Young duckbills traveled with their parents, who protected them.

Each duckbill had a head crest that served as a trumpet. The crest was made of hollow bones and filled with air tubes. When a duckbill breathed air into the tubes, they vibrated and made a sound: *honk!* This may have been a very noisy scene.

The duckbilled *Hypacrosaurus* had a handsome head crest. This plant-eater lived in large herds. Adult males probably had the largest crests. Juveniles had the smallest. The crests helped members identify each other—by sight and sound.

Meet the most gigantic crocodile that ever lived! The *Sarcosuchus* was not a dinosaur at all, but a forty-foot long reptile. It lay in wait along riverbanks and snatched unwary prey—including big dinosaurs! This *Ouranosaurus* herd had better watch out. *Ouranosaurus* had a sail made of spiny bones covered in skin. When the sail faced toward the sun, it absorbed heat and warmed the dinosaur's body. When it faced into a breeze, the sail helped the animal's body cool down.

Archaeopteryx (below) was a dinosaur that looked like a bird. This animal is one reason scientists think that birds came from a family of dinosaurs. Like the dinosaurs, *Archaeopteryx* had teeth. But it also had long feathers and could probably fly. Small meat-eaters like *Protoarcheopteryx* (bottom right) and *Dromaeosaurus* (top right) may have looked like the earliest birds. Scientists think they probably had feathers, too.

Polacanthus was an armored dinosaur. It looked like a walking tank. It was covered in bony knobs and spikes that protected it against meat-eaters. *Polacanthus* could not run away from its enemies. All that armor made it very slow and heavy.

The plated dinosaurs (box) were probably not very smart. Inside their small, narrow heads were some teeny-tiny brains. The row of bony plates down their backs looked impressive, but did not offer much protection. The plates were too fragile. Their long, sharp tail spikes, on the other hand, could be deadly. When the plated dinosaur swung its tail, even the largest meat-eater had to get out of the way! Clockwise, starting in the upper left, these plated dinosaurs are: *Stegosaurus*, *Tuojiangosaurus*, *Dacentrurus*, *Lexovisaurus*, and *Kentrosaurus*.

Coelophysis was one of the earliest dinosaurs. This small meat-eater lived 210 million years ago, in what is now New Mexico. It was fast and light, with hollow, birdlike bones. It traveled in packs, hunting lizards and other small reptiles. With its three-fingered hands, it could grab insects or dig in the earth for worms.

A vicious, horned *Ceratosaurus* (below) threatens a *Brachiosaurus*. *Ceratosaurus* had powerful hind limbs for running fast. It had small front limbs for tearing into prey. A huge plant-eater like *Brachiosaurus* would have been one of its favorite foods.

But *Brachiosaurus* was able to defend itself. It had a long powerful neck and whiplike tail. If it stepped on *Ceratosaurus*, it could squash him.

Tyrannosaurus rex was a giant meat-eating machine. Its huge head was filled with more than 50 teeth. These could tear off great chunks of flesh and bone with a single bite. Here an adult *T. rex* brings down a duckbilled *Corythosaurus*. A youngster moves in for the meal.

In the box are *T. rex* (center) and its relatives: *Daspletosaurus* (left) and *Tarbosaurus* (right). They were the largest, most terrible land hunters that ever lived. These three meat-eaters lived at about the same time, but in different places.

The smallest meat-eating dinosaurs had a lot in common. They were quick, light, and fairly smart. They may also have been warm-blooded like mammals and birds. And—most amazing of all—many of them had feathers! *Sinosauropteryx* (top left) was covered with short, feathery down. *Caudipteryx* (middle left) and *Microraptor* (bottom left) had a fan of feathers on the tail and forelimbs. None of these dinosaurs could fly, though. The fluffy feathers helped keep them warm.

Ornithomimus was an unusual kind of meat-eater. It had no teeth! Instead, it had a horny beak like that of an ostrich. Like the modern ostrich, it ate all kinds of food—from seeds and leaves to eggs and lizards. *Ornithomimus*, smart and speedy, was a skillful hunter. With its large eyes, it could spot prey—and enemies—from a distance. And it could run up to 50 miles per hour.

Neovenator was a huge meat-eater with a thick neck and knife-edged teeth. Fast and agile, it probably hunted in packs. Even a giant plant-eater would be in danger from a group of *Neovenators*!

Big meat-eaters like *Neovenator*, *Tarbosaurus* (left box) and *Gasosaurus* (right box) had powerful hind limbs for chasing after prey. And they had short, clawed forelimbs for ripping prey apart. They were good hunters, but they probably also ate animals that were already dead.

A pack of *Deinonychus* tear into a *Tenontosaurus*. The attackers had special weapons—a savage, six-inch claw on each foot! *Deinonychus* was a quick thinker, fast runner, and high jumper. Because it moved so fast, some scientists think that it was warm-blooded.

Deinonychus probably hunted in packs, like wolves. They would circle around their prey, surrounding it on all sides. Then, at just the right moment—they would leap! The poor victim did not have a chance.

The *Baronyx* was an unusual dinosaur. It had a long, narrow jaw with many pointed teeth. Its snout looked like that of a crocodile. And, just like a crocodile, *Baronyx* caught and ate fish. It waited by the shores of streams and rivers to snatch fish in its jaws or huge claws. Its thumb claw was more than 12 inches long!

DINO FUN FACTS

The dinosaurs lived for about 160 million years. The time during which they lived is called the Mesozoic (mess-uh-ZO-ick) Era. This, in turn, is broken into three different periods of time. They are:

- The Triassic Period—245 million years ago to 205 million years ago.
- The Jurassic Period—205 million years ago to 140 million years ago.
- The Cretaceous period—140 million years ago to 65 million years ago.

Different groups of dinosaurs lived in each of these three time periods. Listed below is more information about each of the fabulous dinosaurs in this book.

Allosaurus (pp. 8–9)
(AL-uh-saw-rus)
Meaning of name: Other lizard
Length: 42 feet
Weight: 1–2 tons
Food: Large plant eaters
Where: North America, Africa, Australia, maybe Asia
When: Late Jurassic

Apatosaurus (pp. 10–11)
(a-PAT-uh-SAW-rus)
Meaning of name: Deceptive reptile
Length: 69–75½ feet
Weight: 25–35 tons
Food: Plants
Where: Southwestern USA, Mexico
When: Late Jurassic

Baronyx (p. 30)
(BAR-ee-ON-icks)
Meaning of name: Heavy claw
Length: 32 feet
Weight: 2 tons
Food: Animal and fish
Where: England
When: Early Cretaceous

Brachiosaurus (p. 21)
(BRACK-ee-uh-SAW-rus)
Meaning of name: Arm reptile
Length: 80–85 feet
Weight: 50–80 tons
Food: Plants
Where: Western North America, south western Europe, North and East Africa
When: Late Jurassic to Early Cretaceous

Caudipteryx (p. 24)
(caw-DIP-ter-icks)
Meaning of name: Tail feather
Length: 31 inches
Weight: 11 pounds
Food: Small animals and insects
Where: China
When: Early Cretaceous

Ceratosaurus (pp. 10, 21)
(sir-RAT-uh-SAW-rus)
Meaning of name: Horned reptile
Length: 31 feet
Weight: 2 tons
Food: Animals
Where: USA, Portugal, maybe Africa
When: Late Jurassic

Coelophysis (p. 20)
(see-low-FY-sis)
Meaning of name: Hollow form
Length: 9 feet
Weight: 100 pounds
Food: Small animals, insects, fish
Where: Eastern USA, New Mexico
When: Late Triassic

Compsognathus (p. 17)
(komp-son-NAY-thus)
Meaning of name: Elegant jaw
Length: 4½ feet
Weight: 6½ pounds
Food: Small animals and insects
Where: Germany, France
When: Late Jurassic

Daspletosaurus (p. 23)
(dass-PLEET-uh-SAW-rus)
Meaning of name: Frightful reptile
Length: 30–33 feet
Weight: 3 tons
Food: Animals
Where: Canada
When: Late Cretaceous

Deinonychus (pp. 28–29)
(die-NON-ih-kuss)
Meaning of name: Terrible claw
Length: 10 feet
Weight: 175 pounds
Food: Animals
Where: Western USA
When: Mid-Cretaceous

Diplodocus (pp. 8–9)
(di-PLOD-uh-kus)
Meaning of name: Double beam
Length: 90 feet
Weight: 12 tons
Food: Plants
Where: North America
When: Late Jurassic

Dromaeosaurus (p. 17)
(dro-MAY-uh-SAW-rus)
Meaning of name: Running reptile
Length: 5½ feet
Weight: 100 pounds
Food: Animals
Where: Western USA, Canada
When: Late Cretaceous

Gasosaurus (p. 26)
(GAS-uh-SAW-rus)
Meaning of name: Gas reptile
Length: 12 feet
Weight: 350 pounds
Food: Animals
Where: China
When: Middle Jurassic

Hypacrosaurus (p. 14)
(hi-PACK-roe-saw-rus)
Meaning of name: Below the top lizard
Length: 30 feet
Weight: 3–4 tons
Food: Plants
Where: North America
When: Late Cretaceous

Iguanodon (p. 3)
(ih-GWAN-uh-don)
Meaning of name: Iguana tooth
Length: 33 feet
Weight: 4–5 tons
Food: Plants
Where: England, Europe, Northern
    Africa, North America
When: Early to mid-Cretaceous

Lambeosaurus (pp. 12–13)
(LAM-bee-uh-SAW-rus)
Meaning of name: Lambe's lizard
Length: Up to 40 feet
Weight: 5–6 tons
Food: Plants
Where: Western USA, Canada, Mexico
When: Late Cretaceous

Maiasaura (pp. 6–7)
(MY-a-SAW-ra)
Meaning of name: Good mother lizard
Length: 29½ feet
Weight: 3–4 tons
Food: Plants
Where: Western USA, Canada
When: Late Cretaceous

Microraptor gui (p. 24)
(MY-crow-rap-tor)
Meaning of name: Gu's small raptor
Length: 3.3 feet
Food: Small animals, insects
Where: China
When: Early Cretaceous

Neovenator (pp. 26–27)
(nee-OWE-ven-uh-tor)
Meaning of name: New hunter

Length: 33 feet
Weight: 1–2 tons
Food: Animals
Where: England
When: Early Cretaceous

Ornithomimus (pp. 24–25)
(or-nith-uh-MY-mus)
Meaning of name: Bird mimic
Length: 13–20 feet
Weight: 290–350 pounds
Food: Plants, insects, small animals
Where: Western USA
When: Late Cretaceous

Ouranosaurus (p.15)
(oo-RAN-uh-SAW-rus)
Meaning of name: Valiant lizard
Length: 23 feet
Weight: 3–4 tons
Food: Plants
Where: Africa (Niger)
When: Early and mid-Cretaceous

Parasaurolophus (pp. 12–13)
(PAR-uh-SAW-ruh-LOW-fus)
Meaning of name: Beside crested reptile
Length: 40 feet
Weight: 2–3 tons
Food: Plants
Where: Western USA, Canada
When: Late Cretaceous

Polacanthus (pp. 18–19)
(pole-uh-CAN-thus)
Meaning of name: Many spikes
Length: 13–16½ feet
Weight: 1–2 tons
Food: Plants
Where: Southern England, Europe
When: Early Cretaceous

Protoarcheopteryx (p. 17)
(PRO-toe-ark-ee-OP-ter-icks)
Meaning of name: Before Archaeopteryx
Length: 28 inches
Weight: 1–2 pounds
Food: Small animals, insects, plants

Where: China
When: Early Cretaceous

Sinosauropteryx (p. 24)
(SIGH-no-saw-OP-ter-icks)
Meaning of name: Chinese reptile wing
Length: 4 feet
Weight: 6½ pounds
Food: Small animals
Where: China
When: Middle Cretaceous

Stegosaurus (p. 19)
(STEG-uh-SAW-rus)
Meaning of name: Plated lizard
Length: 26–29 feet
Weight: 2–3 tons
Food: Plants
Where: Western USA, Europe
When: Late Jurassic

Tarbosaurus (pp. 23, 26)
(TAR-buh-SAW-rus)
Meaning of name: Terrible lizard
Length: 46 feet
Weight: 4 tons
Food: Animals
Where: Mongolia
When: Late Cretaceous

Tenontosaurus (pp. 28–19)
(ten-ON-tuh-SAW-rus)
Meaning of name: Sinew reptile
Length: 24 feet
Weight: 1 ton
Food: Plants
Where: USA
When: Early Cretaceous

Tyrannosaurus rex (pp. 11, 22–23)
(tie-RAN-uh-SAW-rus REKS)
Meaning of name: Tyrant reptile
Length: 50 feet
Weight: 6 tons
Food: Animals
Where: Western North America
When: Late Cretaceous